Hammer your Grammar

Workbook Grade 4

Om
KIDZ
An imprint of Om Books International

POETRY TIME

Read the poem, circle the nouns and write their type.

Polly the parrot,

_____

Was a pirate at sea.

_____

And she was happier,

_____

Than any pirate could be.

_____

She saw such crazy sights,

_____

Like dolphins wearing rings,

_____

And whales who liked to gobble,

_____

Mouldy green things.

_____

POETRY TIME

She met crazy dogs,

_____

Who lived on rows of trees.

_____

And funny little monkeys,

_____

With guitars on their knees.

_____

Then one day she met a parrot,

_____

Who was both handsome and jolly.

_____

And that was the last we saw,

_____

Of our beloved pirate Polly.

_____

JUNGLE SCRAMBLE

Fill in the letters to complete the crossword. Unscramble the letters on the leaves to get your clues.

rtoligaal

ndaap

rlisuqre

cuihenarr

tra

oanrc

kle

ele

doaerlp

aleeg

tetro

ldtpeao

THE PATH TO PRONOUNS

Circle the right word in the bracket to complete the path correctly.

(Us, We) plucked fresh herbs from the woods.

Will you let (us, we) help you cook?

(You, Your, Yours, You're) the best friend I've ever had.

(You, Your, Yours, You're) was the best birthday party.

(You, Your, Yours, You're) coat is so soft!

(You, Your, Yours, You're) are very special!

PUNCTUATION JUNCTION

Help the animals place the correct punctuation and reach the forest junction.

the teacher says look children theres a rainbow in the sky the poet william wordsworth said my heart leaps up when I behold a rainbow in the sky the colours of the rainbow are violet indigo blue green yellow orange and red

the children all shout in delight yes they want to catch a rainbow which of course they cant have you ever tried to catch a rainbow

as the children try to walk into the forest their teacher exclaims look what a pretty sight this is there are baby birds in that nest

back at school the children were asked would you like to go again write a short story about your school trip

Forest

PUZZLING!

Danny the Dinosaur wants to know if the underlined words are adjectives or adverbs. Write the correct answer on the blanks.

Look at the <u>bubbly</u> monkey jumping <u>up and down</u> the tree.

_____

Oh! See the <u>graceful</u> galloping of the <u>enchanting</u> mare.

_____

The <u>big</u> redwood trees are <u>remarkably</u> tall!

_____

The <u>black</u> koel sings <u>beautifully</u>.

_____

<u>White</u> pandas look <u>cute</u>.

_____

That <u>small</u> puppy was born <u>yesterday</u>.

_____

_____

KELLIE'S COMPARISON CLASS

Help Kelly the Kangaroo prepare for her comparison class by filling the chart below.

Positive	Comparative	Superlative
beautiful		
	farther / further	
		oldest / eldest
lazy		
large		
	larger	
		sweetest
	more intelligent	
thin		
	younger	

TENSE TALES

Help Rocky the Rabbit fill in the blanks using the correct tense of the words in brackets.

We must _____ awareness about our ecology. (to build)

Jungle Book will make you _____ in love with animals. (to fall)

He _____ that he would never ill treat the dog again. (to say)

Have you _____ the lamp by the sleeping cubs? (to see)

The ducks _____ in the lake last evening. (to swim)

She _____ the carrots for her pet rabbits so she could give them later. (to save)

We stopped them from _____ the trees. (to cut)

Have you _____ past the woods in the morning? It is a beautiful feeling. (to walk)

VERB WORM

Help Whizzy the Worm fill in the blanks with the correct verb.

- Jack and Jill _____ environmentalists.
  (is / are)

- Either Jack or Jill _____ an environmentalist.
  (is / are)

- Black wattle, candle nut and red tulip nut _____ in rainforests. (grow / grows)

- My dog and cat _____ together.
  (play / plays)

- Her pets and mine _____ come for a walk.
  (has / have)

- Neither Jack nor Jill _____ an environmentalist.
  (is / are)

- In forests, big animals and small ones _____ in unity.
  (live / lives)

The big and the small _____ forward in times of need. (come / comes)

Neither she nor her cubs _____ come to the clearing. (has / have)

Either a ball or a few rings _____ used to train animals in a circus. (is / are)

There _____ a hundred things that animals do in a day. (is / are)

The majority _____ in favour of the nature walk. (is / are)

She _____ the birds every day. (feed / feeds)

are   have
plays   feeds
lives
comes

CATTY CLAUSE

Jimmy the Jungle Cat wants to learn about clauses. Can you underline them in the following sentences? A clause is a part of a sentence with a subject and a predicate of its own.

If you do not take care, you will have no water.

When the sun sets, birds go to sleep.

Here is the pet that you wanted.

It was the storm that knocked some trees down.

I thought that today would be a sunny day.

Can you see the birds by the lake?

SENTENCE SORTING

Help Sammy the Snake categorise these sentences by ticking the correct boxes.

The big brown bear ran after the pot of honey.

☐ Simple   ☐ Complex   ☐ Compound

Many people watched the movie Jungle Book and liked it.

☐ Simple   ☐ Complex   ☐ Compound

My dog and cat slept after they drank milk.

☐ Simple   ☐ Complex   ☐ Compound

Before we begin our journey, let's read about the trip.

☐ Simple   ☐ Complex   ☐ Compound

After dark, the owls will hoot.

☐ Simple   ☐ Complex   ☐ Compound

Although she was unwell, she attended class.

☐ Simple   ☐ Complex   ☐ Compound

THE GRASSHOPPER AND THE ANT

Fill in their conversation with the right question words.

who   where   why   what   whom   how   when   which   whose

Grasshopper

Ant

_____ are you doing?

Gathering food for the winter. _____ don't you do the same?

_____ thinks about winter now?

I do. When winter comes _____ will you go?

_____ is winter? Far away!

_____ will you ask for food then?

_____ is the right thing to do?

_____ house will you knock at when winter arrives?

VERB ALERT

Jinx the Jackal stole verbs from the sentences. Can you return them to the correct places?

We _____ to respect animals and plants.

_____ I use your pictures for my project?

We _____ take the bus for our field trip tomorrow, although it is not certain.

The forest officer _____ be taking down our names.

Please, _____ you sit down and explain the life-cycle of a butterfly?

I _____ show you the way to the forest river.

ought   may   might

will   would   shall

JUNGLE JUMBLE

The animals have a test to complete! Help them finish it.

Match and complete.

Let's write a _____ on animal conservation.

Let's _____ after lunch.

The mosquito _____ him.

May I have a _____ of sugar in my coffee?

| bit |
| bit |
| play |
| play |

Fill in the blanks with homographs.

| wound, present |

Are all the students _____ today?

The teacher will _____ the marks now.

The rope was _____ around the snake.

He received a small _____ while playing.

Choose the right option.

We will not _____ water.
(waste / waist)

May I go for the play _____?
(too / to)

The horse _____ away without its master.
(rode / road)

The _____ spoke to the parents.
(principle / principal)

Fill in the blanks.

The _____ ran away with the honey.
(bear / bare)

_____ of them know their way to the lake. (nun / none)

The dolphin lives in the deep blue _____.
(sea / see)

OPPOSITES ATTRACT

An oxymoron is a phrase that uses two words with opposite meanings. Match the lion's words to the tiger's and make some oxymorons.

Lion	Tiger
all	sweat
detailed	alone
cold	summary
half	fool
wise	crowd
small	full

DIRECTLY INDIRECT

Joky the Jackal loves changing conversations around.
Can you help him rewrite these sentences using
indirect speech?

The fox said, "I want those grapes!"

_____

_____

The shepherd thought, "I am bored!"

_____

_____

The grasshopper said to the ant, "Why
are you working so hard?"

_____

_____

The mouse asked the lion, "Was I
not right?"

_____

_____

PEPPERING PREPOSITIONS

Help Dingo the Dog fill in the blanks with prepositions.

My dog jumped _____ of the window and _____ my car.

Walk _____ the corridor and you will find the sleeping kitten.

The circus elephant climbed _____ the stairs.

The rabbit jumped _____ the fence and ran _____ the garden.

The bull ran _____ the spectators.

The cub saw place _____ two trees and rested there.

towards   along   out   of   up   over   into   between

ANIMAL ANALOGIES

Complete the analogies for the animals below.

A cow is to milk as a _____ is to eggs.

Fleet is to ships as _____ is to elephants.

Bird is to feather as _____ is to wool.

Bird is to fly as fish is to _____.

Duck is to duckling as horse is to _____.

PATRICK'S PROVERB STORE

Patrick the Parrot sells proverbs in the jungle. Help him sort them out by choosing the correct meaning for each one.

Bull in a China shop.

There's a shop in China with a bull in it. ☐

There are shops in China which have bulls. ☐

To be very clumsy. ☐

Rats abandoning a sinking ship.

When a ship sinks, there are rats on it. ☐

Rats live on ships. ☐

People who are not loyal. ☐

Smell a rat.

To be suspicious of something or get the feeling that something is wrong. ☐

Find the smell of a rat. ☐

See a rat and try to find it. ☐

Don't cut down the tree that gives you shade.

Trees give shade so we must not cut them down. ☐

Never cut a tree. ☐

Never harm or hurt something or someone that does good to you. ☐

If you call one wolf, you invite the pack.

One bad habit leads to another. ☐

One wolf calls another. ☐

A group of wolves is called a pack. ☐

Lock the stable door after the horse has run.

After the horse runs, lock the stable door. ☐

To prevent something that has already happened from happening. ☐

Don't lock stable doors, or the horses will run. ☐

SIMILE SURPRISE

Match the similes to the correct animals.

As fresh as a

As cunning as a

As innocent as a

As happy as a

As wise as an

As hungry as a

A stubborn as a

bear

owl

lark

lamb

fox

mule

daisy

Read the sentences and identify the parts of speech for the underlined words.

Since this afternoon, the dog has been barking.

_____

Since there's nothing else to do, let's go for a walk.

_____

I have not seen my cat ever since.

_____

Well, what an unusual bird!

_____

Is the tiger well now?

_____

The bird fell in the well.

_____

Create a jungle story based on Otto Owl's outline.

Animals in a jungle – constant fights – no one likes each other – jungle lake goes dry – no water – animals look for a solution – some animals team up and bring water from a nearby jungle – everyone stops fighting.

_____
_____
_____
_____
_____
_____
_____
_____
_____
_____
_____
_____

PEPPER'S POETRY

Help Pepper the Penguin write a poem about himself. Use the rhyming words from the ice cubes.

_____

_____

_____

_____

_____

_____

_____

_____

_____

_____

_____

fat-sat

bit-fit

swim-him

food-mood

new-few

smile-while

friend-end

POEM PROBLEMS

Let's read Jinny's poem and answer the questions that follow.

Jinny the giraffe,
was tall and thin.
And what she loved,
was to always win.

She would win at basketball,
and star gazing too.
She would win a free ice cream,
on a picnic to the zoo.

She would win at playing catch,
or a clever game of chess.
And at costume parties,
she would win for the best dress.

But Jinny's friends didn't hate her.
She was actually quite nice.
For every time she won,
she shared her lovely prize.

Who was Jinny?

_____

_____

What was she good at?

_____

_____

Did the other animals hate her for being good?

_____

_____

What did she do with her prizes?

_____

_____

What do you learn from Jinny?

_____

_____

A JUNGLE'S TALE

If you were a jungle, what would you be like? Write an essay about yourself as a jungle.